CORNERSTONES OF FREEDOM™

ENVIRONMENTAL PROTECTION

BY WIL MARA

CHILDREN'S PRESS®

An Imprint of Scholastic Inc.

New York   Toronto   London   Auckland   Sydney

Mexico City   New Delhi   Hong Kong

Danbury, Connecticut

BRINGING HISTORY to LIFE

Content Consultant
James Marten, PhD
Professor and Chair, History Department
Marquette University
Milwaukee, Wisconsin

Library of Congress Cataloging-in-Publication Data
Mara, Wil.
  Environmental protection / by Wil Mara.
      p. cm.—(Cornerstones of freedom)
  Includes bibliographical references and index.
  ISBN 978-0-531-23603-1 (lib. bdg.)—ISBN 978-0-531-21961-4 (pbk.)
  1. Environmental protection—United States—Juvenile
literature. 2. United States—Environmental conditions—Juvenile
literature. I. Title.
  TD170.15.M35 2013
  363.70973—dc23   2012034321

All rights reserved. Published in 2013 by Children's Press, an imprint of
Scholastic Inc.
Printed in the United States of America 113

SCHOLASTIC, CHILDREN'S PRESS, CORNERSTONES OF FREEDOM™,
and associated logos are trademarks and/or registered trademarks of
Scholastic Inc.

1 2 3 4 5 6 7 8 9 10 R 22 21 20 19 18 17 16 15 14 13

Photographs © 2013: Alamy Images/Jim West: 27; AP Images: 50 (Arctic
National Wildlife Refuge), 36, 57 top (Charles Tasnadi), 4 top, 51 (Gerald
Herbert), 34, 37 (Henry Burroughs), 6 (North Wind Picture Archives), 42
(Ron Edmonds), 55 (Tom Uhlman); Corbis Images/Bettmann: 25; Getty
Images/Arthur Schatz/Time & Life Pictures: 30; Library of Congress: 10
(Geo. F. Parlow), 16 (George Grantham Bain Collection), 7 (Mathew B.
Brady), 15 (U.S. Forest Service), 17 (Underwood & Underwood), 18, 56;
Photo Researchers: 19 (Farrell Grehan), back cover (Pierre Huguet),
22 (Science Source); Redux/Rien Zilvold/Hollandse Hoogte: cover;
Superstock, Inc.: 5 bottom, 44 (Ambient Images Inc.), 12, 24, 26 (Everett
Collection), 2, 3, 28 (John Hyde/Alaska Stock), 35 (Minden Pictures), 48
(Stock Connection), 11, 39 (Visions of America), 4 bottom, 47 (Wayne
Lynch/All Canada Photos), 13, 41, 57 bottom; The Image Works: 33 (Charles
Gatewood), 20 (H. Armstrong Roberts/ClassicStock), 5 top, 32 (Jacques
Boyer/Roger-Viollet), 54 (Mike Kahn/GreenStockMedia), 45 (Peter
Hvizdak), 14 (Photo12), 8 (Print Collector/HIP), 23 (Scherl/SZ Photo).

Maps by XNR Productions, Inc.

Did you know that studying history can be fun?

BRING HISTORY TO LIFE by becoming a history investigator. Examine the evidence (primary and secondary source materials); cross-examine the people and witnesses. Take a look at what was happening at the time—but be careful! What happened years ago might suddenly become incredibly interesting and change the way you think!

Contents

The Domino Effect

Early settlers chopped down trees to make fires and build their homes.

When European settlers first journeyed across the Atlantic Ocean in their quest for a better life in America, they carried with them the belief that the resources of the land should be used for the improvement of each person's life. But it wasn't long before the growing demands of the **colonies** began to have a negative effect on the natural world.

GEORGE PERKINS MARSH HELPED FOUND

The settlers cleared forests to make room for their farms. They used the wood from the fallen trees to construct buildings and create useful products. However, such activities destroyed the homes of many plant and animal species. A domino effect followed, upsetting nature's delicate balance. For example, birds that ate insect pests would move off to other areas when their treetop homes were removed. This gave the insects a chance to multiply in greater numbers and attack the colonists' crops.

In 1864, former U.S. representative George Perkins Marsh published a book called *Man and Nature*. It spelled out the many environmental problems that humans were causing. It also explained how continued abuse of the wilderness could ultimately lead to America's downfall. Many people consider Marsh's book to be the beginning of the U.S. environmental movement. Since its publication, millions have worked to protect the natural world from damage caused by humans.

George Perkins Marsh was one of the first Americans to write about environmental issues.

THE SMITHSONIAN INSTITUTION IN 1846.

CHAPTER 1

THE FIRST AGE OF AMERICAN ENVIRONMENTALISM

The United States became much more industrialized during the second half of the 19th century.

THE FIRST PERIOD IN AMERICAN history when both the government and the people began to make significant moves toward environmental protection occurred in the years leading up to the 20th century. America was becoming more **industrialized**. This made it more dependent on natural resources such as coal, oil, wood, and metal. Such resources are grown or developed through natural processes. Removing or altering too many can cause major problems in the environment. As a result, environmental problems developed on a scale never seen before. This made the public aware of environmental issues, setting the stage for a new social movement.

Henry David Thoreau's *Walden* is a classic environmental text that remains popular today.

Getting the Public Involved

Man and Nature was not the only book to get people thinking about the environment in the mid-1800s. Marsh's book was practical and direct in its approach. But Henry David Thoreau's *Walden*, published in 1854, offered a more abstract perspective of man's relationship with the environment. Thoreau was born in Concord, Massachusetts, in July 1817. He grew to develop a deep appreciation for nature as well as a love of writing. In the summer of 1845, he combined these passions when he built a tiny home in Massachusetts along the forested shores of Walden Pond. He stayed there for roughly two years. During that time, he kept a written record of his experiences living in the wilderness.

A FIRSTHAND LOOK AT
WALDEN

Henry David Thoreau's original intent while at Walden Pond was to return to a simpler lifestyle that was free of all distractions. *Walden*, the book he wrote during his stay in the woods, became an important inspiration for many environmentalists. See page 60 for a link to read it online.

Walden, Man and Nature, and early outdoors magazines such as *Field & Stream* made the public aware of the natural world's beauty and practical importance. Numerous paintings and the relatively new technology of photography also filled people with a greater respect for nature. Public attitudes toward the natural world began to change.

The woods around Walden Pond inspired Thoreau to create his best-known work.

The Progressive Era

These changes began to take root during one of the most important periods in American history—the Progressive Era. Spanning from the 1890s to the 1920s, this period saw an evolution in the way people viewed many issues. They began to search for more **efficient** ways of using natural resources. Most people felt that they should be allowed to harvest resources as they always had. But there was a greater emphasis on making sure these resources would be available for future generations. For example, if a hundred trees were cut down, a hundred new trees would be planted to replace them.

During the Progressive Era, people continued harvesting natural resources, but concentrated on finding ways to be less wasteful.

Preservationists wanted to ensure that outdoor areas remained in their natural state.

This approach didn't satisfy everyone who cared about the natural world. Those who embraced it were known as **conservationists**. They believed in conserving resources for future use. Others, known as **preservationists**, believed that the environment should be left largely undisturbed and appreciated only for its beauty. This difference in opinion between the conservationists and preservationists would cause problems in the years ahead. During the Progressive Era, however, conservationists had a much stronger influence.

Theodore Roosevelt (front) was an avid hunter and conservationist.

Roosevelt and Pinchot

Perhaps the most powerful figure to support
conservation during the Progressive Era was President
Theodore Roosevelt. Roosevelt had loved the natural
world all his life. He studied biology at Harvard College
and spent time as a rancher in the Dakotas. He later
explored the Yellowstone region of the United States and
the Amazonian rain forests of South America.

During his time as president (1901–1909), Roosevelt
made conservation an important priority. He created the
United States Forest Service, which today is responsible
for the management and protection of nearly 200
million acres (80 million hectares) of land. He also

established the Antiquities Act in 1906. This act granted the president the power to designate segments of public land as protected areas. Environmentally destructive activities are legally barred in these areas. Roosevelt used the new law to protect such locations as Devils Tower in Wyoming and the Grand Canyon in Arizona.

Roosevelt (left) worked closely with Gifford Pinchot (right) to develop a conservation program in the United States.

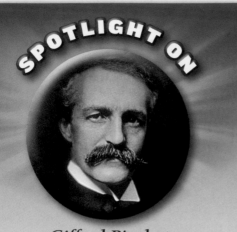

Gifford Pinchot

Gifford Pinchot was born in Connecticut in 1865. His father had been in the business of harvesting lumber for land development and eventually had deep regrets about causing so much environmental damage. As a result, he encouraged his son to go into a career where he could focus on conservation. Pinchot attended Yale University and graduated in 1889. Afterward, his passion for the natural world led him to further studies at a forestry school in France. He would later use the skills learned there to become one of the United States' most important conservationists.

President Roosevelt's greatest ally in these conservation efforts was a man named Gifford Pinchot. Pinchot was an expert in forestry management who had been selected by President Grover Cleveland to develop a conservation plan for woodlands in the western United States. He became head of the federal government's Division of Forestry in 1898, under President William McKinley. In 1905, Roosevelt placed him in charge of all national forests.

Pinchot's vision for the nation's natural resources was much the same as Roosevelt's. With Pinchot's help, Roosevelt was able to place millions of acres of land under the protection of the U.S. Forest Service by the end of his presidency.

John Muir (right) and Theodore Roosevelt (left) worked together to expand environmentalism in the United States.

John Muir and the Sierra Club

Another leading environmental figure during the Progressive Era was John Muir. Muir was born in Scotland in 1838. He moved with his family to the United States in 1849. The Muirs started a farm, where John's passion for nature began to flourish. He attended college but did not make much progress toward a degree, as he only took courses in subjects that interested him. In 1867, he began his first serious exploration of nature, a 1,000-mile (1,609-kilometer) walk from Indiana to Florida. Muir traveled along only the wildest and most undeveloped routes.

In early 1868, Muir went to Yosemite in Northern California, and was awestruck by its beauty. He spent the next three years living in the area. He built a cabin in the wilderness and lived on a diet of fruits and vegetables. Muir played a key role in convincing Congress to make Yosemite a national park in 1890.

In 1892, Muir helped form a preservationist organization called the Sierra Club. He was the club's first president, and held the position until he died in 1914. The Sierra Club fought for the preservation of untouched wilderness areas. This placed it at odds with the beliefs of Roosevelt and Pinchot. Muir and Pinchot were friends for a time. However, Muir became frustrated with Pinchot's willingness to take advantage of natural

John Muir and his Sierra Club were strong believers in preservation.

resources. Muir knew humankind needed these resources, but he wanted their use kept to a minimum.

Muir lost what was perhaps his greatest environmental battle when he failed to prevent the U.S. government from building a dam in the Hetch Hetchy Valley area of Yosemite. The dam blocked the Tuolumne River, flooding the valley and making a reservoir. Muir considered this a destructive act against a beautiful natural area. The growing population of San Francisco needed water, however, so the conservationists won the fight. Muir was furious with the then president Woodrow Wilson for supporting the dam project.

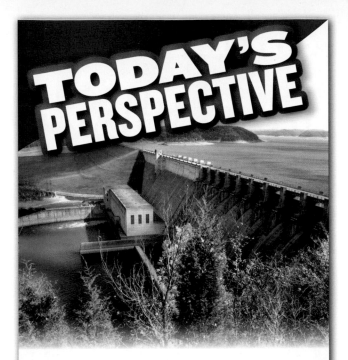

TODAY'S PERSPECTIVE

A century after construction started on the dam at Hetch Hetchy Valley, the Sierra Club is still determined to remove it and restore the area to its original beauty. In 2004, then president of the Sierra Club Larry Fahn told members, "A fitting tribute to John Muir would be for us to find the wisdom and the will to restore the grandeur of Hetch Hetchy Valley, in the early 21st century, for our families and all future generations." The club insists that the dam can be removed without nearby residents losing their water supply. Sierra Club supporters argue that there are many other water sources in the area.

CHAPTER 2

WHAT GOES AROUND COMES AROUND

Damage to the environment can affect the food that people eat.

THE ENVIRONMENTAL MOVEMENT focused largely on responsible use of natural resources during the Progressive Era. In the years that followed, it shifted more toward the damage that was being caused by industrial growth and how that damage affected humans. People began to realize that harm to the environment could find its way into their kitchens, onto their dinner plates, and inside their bodies. They began to understand that humans themselves were part of the environment and that all livings things were connected in significant ways.

Alice Hamilton exposed the environmental damage being caused by large industrial companies.

Growing Problems for a Growing Nation

One of the earliest efforts to raise public awareness of how a damaged environment could affect people came in Alice Hamilton's 1925 book *Industrial Poisons in the United States.* Hamilton had received a medical degree in 1893 and became interested in the negative impact that dangerous workplaces could have on employees. She also called attention to the serious effects of industrial waste on the natural world. Her work pointed out how often environmental damage came back around to impact the public. Poisoned water, soil, and other resources could all harm humans. With the continued growth of industry, many of the problems being caused by factories were going unnoticed until Hamilton wrote about them. The book also helped to define one of the major conflicts of the environmental movement: environmentalists versus big businesses.

The efforts to protect the environment during the Progressive Era were a good start. But they didn't solve all of the problems. One of the most serious issues during the following years was damage to farmlands. Soil in many rural areas was so worn out that it could no longer support crops. Too much farming had drained it of its nutrients. Also, waterways used for **agricultural** purposes

During the Dust Bowl era, soil became too dry for farmers to grow crops.

The Dust Bowl

One of the greatest environmental disasters in American history occurred during the Great Depression. It was known as the Dust Bowl. A series of dust storms swept across the United States' rural farmlands during the 1930s. Over time, farmers had plowed up millions of acres of deeply rooted grasses to make room for crops. These grasses had held moisture in the soil. Without them, the soil quickly turned to dust and began blowing throughout the region. Some dust clouds were so thick that people could see only a few feet in front of them. Farmlands turned into wastelands, and animals died by the thousands. Families were forced to leave their homes and start new lives elsewhere.

had become so polluted that they caused damage to the natural areas they flowed through. Such issues brought about a reduction in farm production. This caused food prices to rise. Many farming families abandoned their exhausted lands and moved to the growing cities in search of better job opportunities. This led to overpopulation problems in the cities. When the **Great Depression** hit America in 1929, many of the farmers who remained in rural areas went from poor to poorer.

Another Roosevelt to the Rescue

President Herbert Hoover made some positive environmental efforts during the heart of the Great Depression. He led

Franklin Roosevelt (far right) made environmental issues, such as improving poor soil, a major part of his 1932 presidential campaign.

a crusade to conserve oil and timber, share water supplies among the states, and fund scientific research for improving farming methods. His successor, Franklin D. Roosevelt, pushed even harder on conservation issues.

Roosevelt began building a track record on environmental issues as governor of New York. He directed state funding to the study of different types of soils, reforesting lands that had been cleared by human activities, and bringing electricity into rural areas. He discussed these achievements during his campaign for president, promising to help poor farmers get their farms going again. Roosevelt, like his distant relative Theodore, believed more in conservation than preservation. He felt that natural resources should be used to benefit people as long as they were used responsibly.

CAMP ROOSEVELT
CIVILIAN·CONSERVATION·CORPS
CAMP No.1

The Civilian Conservation Corps

One of President Franklin Roosevelt's most successful environmental protection efforts was the creation of the Civilian Conservation Corps (CCC). The CCC was launched in 1933. It provided jobs to hundreds of thousands of young men who were out of work because of the Great Depression. The CCC aimed to improve government-owned land across the country. The program was enormously popular with the public. Its workers built hundreds of parks, repaired bridges and dams, and planted millions of trees. They also expanded roadways into formerly undeveloped areas. These new paths permitted better access for future conservation efforts.

Getting the Public More Involved

Roosevelt arranged a conference in Washington, D.C., in 1936 to discuss the future of environmental protection. Many of the organizations invited were not part of the government. They were private groups known as nongovernmental organizations (NGOs). One NGO, the Sierra Club, was well into its fourth decade of operation. Others were much newer. During the conference, a new NGO called the General Wildlife Federation was formed. It was renamed the National Wildlife Federation shortly thereafter, and it continues to this day. These and other NGOs worked to educate people about the environment and motivate them to take action.

More everyday people began to take an active interest in the environment as the NGOs spread their message. Environmental issues were suddenly being discussed not just in the media but also in workplaces, supermarkets, and homes. People began to think more about pollution in their drinking water and the air that they breathed. They also began to consider the idea that energy resources could one day run out and that animal species could become lost forever. Environmentalism was no longer just for scientists, government agencies, and conservationists. It had become the talk of the general public.

NGOs such as the Sierra Club continue to spread awareness of environmental issues today.

Slowly Disappearing

The concept of protecting wild animals was not new, but it had not been given serious consideration in years past. In the early 20th century, the idea that certain species could disappear forever was fairly new and shocking to many people. However, such disappearances were already happening. Habitat destruction, excessive hunting, the growing pet trade, and the widespread use of **pesticides** were all causing serious damage to animal species.

Laws such as the Bald Eagle Protection Act of 1940 were passed in an attempt to address this issue. But these early laws were often ineffective. They were difficult to enforce, and environmental agencies could not devote much effort to the problem. But the public was at least beginning to take notice. Several NGOs would eventually focus their energies on protecting rare animal and plant species.

The Bald Eagle Protection Act has helped ensure that the U.S. national bird continues to thrive in America's wilderness.

A FIRSTHAND LOOK AT
SILENT SPRING

Rachel Carson's *Silent Spring* accused chemical companies of hiding the effects of pesticides from the public. The book was a best seller, and it encouraged many people to think more critically about how human activity affected the natural world. See page 60 for a link to read excerpts of the book online.

Two More Books

In 1949, Aldo Leopold's book *A Sand County Almanac* was published. Leopold, a former employee of the U.S. Forest Service, wrote of the complex relationships among all living things. The book took a more scientific approach to the subject than others of its kind did. In time, it would play a role in moving the environmental movement to a more scientific front.

Rachel Carson's *Silent Spring*, published in 1962, had an even greater impact. Many credit it with becoming one of the launching points of the modern environmental movement. Carson was a biologist with a natural talent for writing. She published many books and articles about the environmental challenges facing the United States. *Silent Spring* focused largely on the devastating effects of pesticides on nature, and in turn on human beings. She made startling claims that the chemical industry was hiding the truth about pollution from the public. The book became a massive best seller and stirred up the environmental movement as it progressed toward its most significant era yet.

CHAPTER 3
RISE AND FALL

During the 1960s, more people began taking an active role in environmental protests.

PUBLIC OUTRAGE TOWARD

environmental problems began to climb to a fever pitch in the early 1960s. It was the beginning of a decade that would see major social changes on many issues. Young people were breaking free of tradition and rejecting the values of their parents. While this approach did not always produce the best results, it did inspire group action of forward-thinking young people that allowed the environmental movement to flourish as it never had before.

The nuclear attacks on Nagasaki (above) and Hiroshima caused long-term damage to the environment in Japan.

Going Nuclear About Going Nuclear

Another new environmental issue began seeping into the public's consciousness in the 1960s. It concerned the growing use of nuclear energy. During World War II (1939–1945), U.S. forces dropped newly developed nuclear bombs on the Japanese cities of Hiroshima and Nagasaki. These attacks brought about Japan's surrender and ended the war. But they were also responsible for killing nearly a quarter of a million people. Some of the victims died immediately. Others perished years later, suffering the effects of **radiation** poisoning.

Following these bombings, the United States continued testing other nuclear devices. These tests resulted in the widespread destruction of the environment where they were undertaken. They also sometimes caused illness and death. One such example was a 1954 test in the Pacific Ocean that poisoned the crew of a Japanese fishing boat.

Some people argued that nuclear power could at least be used to generate electricity inexpensively and provide communities with the electrical power they needed. But accidents at these early nuclear facilities further convinced the public that nuclear power was far too dangerous to be controlled by humans. As a result, an antinuclear effort led by angry citizens became a part of the growing environmental movement.

Many young people joined the protests against nuclear war.

Legislation Overdrive

By the mid-1960s, pressure from a concerned public began forcing elected officials to take real action on environmental issues. New laws and regulations were written and passed at a rapid pace.

One of the first was the Clean Air Act of 1963. This law was designed to reduce the amount of air pollution that came from permanent structures such as homes and factories. The Air Quality Act of 1967 dealt with air pollution caused by automobiles. The Wilderness Act of 1964 was equally important. It protected roughly 9 million acres (3.6 million ha) of land from human disturbance. Perhaps more importantly, it established the legal definition of *wilderness*. This clear definition

President Lyndon Johnson signed the Clean Air Act into law on December 17, 1963.

made it easier for future laws to be written and enforced. In 1968, President Lyndon Johnson signed the National Wild and Scenic Rivers Act. This law protected certain waterways from human development.

The Endangered Species Preservation Act of 1966 was the first major law designed to protect animals that were heading for **extinction**. The act made it illegal for people to capture or kill certain rare animal species. The government also began compiling a list of species that needed protection. This allowed the creation of even stronger

TODAY'S PERSPECTIVE

The 1969 Endangered Species Conservation Act provided an exception that allowed captive-breeding programs to take protected species from the wild. These programs have become very effective in furthering environmental protection. Captive breeding is the process by which a group of animals is allowed to breed and produce young in a controlled environment, such as a zoo. This provides the animals with much safer surroundings than they would have in the wild. Without natural predators or human dangers, their young have a much higher chance of survival. Some species, such as the panda (above), have been saved from extinction solely through captive breeding.

President Nixon (left) chose William Ruckelshaus (right) as the first director of the EPA.

animal protection laws in the future. For example, the 1969 Endangered Species Conservation Act expanded on the 1966 act to protect many additional species.

New Decade, New Ideas

On July 9, 1970, President Richard Nixon ordered the creation of the Environmental Protection Agency (EPA). Before this, different governmental departments had handled different environmental problems. The EPA centralized these efforts and made them more efficient. Nixon planned for the EPA to be an independent agency that could carry out its duties free of influence from the powerful political parties.

Nixon's decision to create the EPA was likely influenced in part by the overwhelming response to the first Earth Day. Earth Day was organized chiefly by Wisconsin senator Gaylord Nelson. Nelson had supported environmental protection throughout his political career. Shortly after returning from a 1969 trip to observe a devastating oil spill in Santa Barbara, California, he suggested an educational event that would draw widespread public attention and inspire people to take action. Nelson wanted

YESTERDAY'S HEADLINES

Immediately after President Nixon created the EPA, he appointed its first director, Indiana congressman William D. Ruckelshaus (above). Ruckelshaus issued a press release stating his goals and intentions. He began by making it clear that the EPA would not be subject to outside influence: "It has no obligation to promote agriculture or commerce; only the critical obligation to protect and enhance the environment."

Ruckelshaus knew, however, that the EPA needed cooperation from other government agencies and private companies: "The job that must be done now to restore and preserve the quality of our air, water, and soil can only be accomplished if this new federal agency works closely with industry and with other levels of government." In the years since, the EPA's relationship with big businesses has sometimes been tense.

schools across the nation to set aside one day to focus on environmental problems. On April 22, 1970, more than 20 million people participated in Nelson's Earth Day event.

And the Laws Keep Coming

Environmental laws continued to roll out of Washington during the 1970s. Public demand for action increased, new NGOs continued to form, environmental law firms became more powerful, and the EPA broadened its influence around the nation.

In 1970, Congress expanded the scope of the Clean Air Act that was first passed in 1963. The additions set limitations on the amount of pollutants a car could produce. The 1972 Noise Control Act addressed the negative effects that extreme noise had on both the natural environment and areas populated by people. It gave the government the power to dictate how much noise vehicles, construction equipment, and other machines could produce. The 1974 Safe Drinking Water Act created strict guidelines for keeping pollutants out of public water supplies. It also led to the banning of lead in the production of water pipes. In 1976, the Toxic Substances Control Act allowed the EPA to monitor companies that manufactured environmentally harmful chemicals. It also allowed the government to punish companies that dumped chemical waste in undeveloped areas.

Losing Some Ground

In the late 1970s, President Jimmy Carter set up forward-thinking environmental programs. These programs included efforts to develop new energy sources such as solar and wind power. President Ronald Reagan, who

President Jimmy Carter supported a variety of environmental protection programs.

succeeded Carter in January 1981, called for funding cuts to these programs. This caused great alarm among environmental groups and activists, who scrambled to increase their power in Washington, D.C. They set up headquarters there, and hired professional **lobbyists**.

Reagan believed that business interests were more important than environmental protection. During his two-term presidency, he permitted numerous energy companies to overrun millions of acres of undeveloped land in search of gas, oil, and coal deposits. Reagan fought to weaken laws such as the Clean Air Act and the Clean Water Act to make it easier for businesses to operate.

Ozone Concerns

One environmental topic that received widespread public attention in the 1980s was the damage being done to the earth's ozone. Ozone is a form of oxygen that exists in a layer around the earth and absorbs potentially harmful radiation given off by the sun.

Scientists began to notice an unusual reduction in the amount of ozone during the 1970s. They discovered that one major cause was that chemicals known as chlorofluorocarbons (CFCs) were being released into the air. CFCs were used mainly in aerosol spray cans. The CFCs that were fired out of each can eventually found their way up to the ozone layer. Over time, this created holes in the ozone. Increased radiation began reaching the earth. This radiation is believed to have caused a variety of problems, including an increase in skin cancer and eye

Ronald Reagan supported business interests over environmental concerns.

disease in humans, the disappearance of entire amphibian colonies, and the widespread destruction of certain crops.

In 1985, nearly two dozen leading industrial nations met in Vienna, Austria, for the Vienna Convention for the Protection of the Ozone Layer. A strategy was outlined for a global effort to eventually phase out the use of CFCs and other substances harmful to ozone. Further details of the plan were laid out in a September 1987 meeting. These plans have since been supported by nations around the world.

CHAPTER 4
TOO MANY COOKS

President Bill Clinton (left) and Vice President Al Gore (right) help clean up flood debris during an Earth Day event in 1996.

THE ENVIRONMENTAL MOVEMENT lost some steam in the 1990s and 2000s. It was unable to regain the momentum it had during the 1960s and 1970s. Much of the movement's focus turned toward the power center of Washington, D.C. There, great things could be achieved with political support, and almost nothing could be accomplished without it. Environmentalists did find some friends in high places, such as President Bill Clinton and Vice President Al Gore. But they also struggled against historic levels of political opposition.

People around the world gathered for parades and festivals on Earth Day 1990.

The Return of Earth Day

The 1990s began on what seemed to be a positive note for the environmental movement with the 20th anniversary of Earth Day on April 22, 1990. This celebration was the first global observance of Earth Day, and it was participated in by more than 200 million people in over 140 nations, inspiring renewed attention to issues such as recycling, nuclear energy, the ozone layer, and illegal dumping. It also established Earth Day as a permanent annual event to be observed around the world every spring thereafter.

Unfortunately, the celebration also hinted at certain fractures in the movement that would become more pronounced in the years ahead. Leaders from different environmental groups disagreed on how to deal with certain issues and how to craft the most effective message for the public. There was also tension caused by the participation of Hewlett-Packard, a technology company that had been guilty of environmentally unfriendly practices in the past. These rifts created the image of an environmental effort that was not as united as it should be.

Global Warming

Global warming has been the environmental issue most often discussed in recent times. Put very simply, global warming is the gradual increase in the average temperature of both the earth's atmosphere and oceans.

Automobiles contribute to global warming by releasing harmful gases into the atmosphere.

Climate change has occurred naturally throughout Earth's history. However, human activity has caused a period of increased warming since at least the 1800s.

The rate of increase has grown dramatically over the past several decades. Scientists are all but certain the cause of this alarming development lies in a severe increase in the amount of **greenhouse gases** accumulating in the earth's atmosphere. Greenhouse gases bring about the greenhouse effect. This process warms the earth when radiation from the sun enters the earth's atmosphere, is absorbed by greenhouse gases, and is then rereleased. Some of the rereleased radiation continues down to the earth's surface and provides heat. The rest returns to space. When the amount of greenhouse gas in the atmosphere increases, so does the amount of radiation that reaches the earth. As a result, the overall temperature of the earth begins to rise.

Several human activities are to blame for this problem. One is the large-scale burning of fossil fuels. These are fuels that form in nature from the remains of prehistoric animals. Coal and petroleum are examples of common fossil fuels. Another cause is deforestation. This is the removal of trees and other plant growth in large areas. Trees absorb carbon dioxide—a common greenhouse gas—from the air and provide oxygen in return. When a tree is cut down, it no longer performs this function. It also releases much of the carbon dioxide it had stored.

There are other causes of global warming as well, including the use of certain fertilizers in farming and the

As sea levels rise, Arctic animals such as polar bears have less living space.

continuing damage to the ozone layer. Experts believe there will be radical changes in weather patterns, an increase in animal and plant extinctions, and an increase in destruction of crops if global warming is not addressed. They also believe desert areas will expand. Fewer regions will be able to support human life. Sea levels have already begun rising steadily, placing portions of land underwater.

World governments, the United Nations, and many environmental NGOs have all cooperated to address global warming in recent years. Strategies have included efforts to develop more environmentally friendly sources of renewable energy. Renewable energy sources include solar, wind, and water power. Other efforts to address global warming include improved methods of reducing the gases released by motorized vehicles and heavy machinery, and the overall reduction of vehicle usage in areas where bicycles and other environmentally friendly means of transportation can be used. In addition, millions of trees

Wind farms can produce electricity without polluting the environment.

have been replanted in deforested areas. The safe use of nuclear power, while frowned upon by many people in the environmental movement, has been identified as a way to produce electricity without significantly increasing the risk of global warming.

The United Nations took the first important step in getting world governments to act together on the global warming issue in 1992 at the United Nations Conference on Environment and Development. During this meeting, leaders began designing a global plan to reduce the amount of greenhouse gases produced by all countries. This was followed in 1997 by the Kyoto Protocol, which required participating nations to reduce their greenhouse emissions each year until acceptable levels were reached. The terms of the Kyoto Protocol remain in effect to this day.

A VIEW FROM ABROAD

The European Union is one of the world leaders in using renewable energy sources. European nations have worked hard to improve the technologies of wind, water, and solar power. Their leaders hope to reduce their dependency on fossil fuels such as oil and to reduce the negative effect of these fuels on the earth's atmosphere. Austria is the leader in this campaign, with more than half of its electrical demands served by forms of renewable energy. Solar panels on the roofs of homes and rows of wind turbines along hilltops are a common sight. A trip through this forward-thinking nation provides the first glimpse of what could be an oil-free future.

Many rare animal species roam the natural environments of the Arctic National Wildlife Refuge in Alaska.

To Drill or Not to Drill

Another controversy in recent years that has pitted the environmental movement against the big business community is the question of whether oil drilling should be permitted in the Arctic National Wildlife Refuge (ANWR). ANWR is 19 million acres (7.7 million ha) of wilderness along the northern coast of Alaska. The great majority of it has remained untouched. However, experts believe it holds as many as 16 billion barrels of oil in one particular section, which has caught the attention of the energy industry. Environmentalists are concerned that drilling to reach these deposits will cause permanent environmental damage.

ANWR has been a protected area since 1980, when President Jimmy Carter signed the Alaska National Interest Lands Conservation Act. This act allowed for drilling but only with approval from Congress. In the years since, oil companies and their political allies have tried hard to get that approval. They almost succeeded in 1996 when both houses of Congress passed a bill to permit the drilling. President Bill Clinton, however, used his power to **veto** the bill. More attempts were made in 2005 and 2009, but they were defeated.

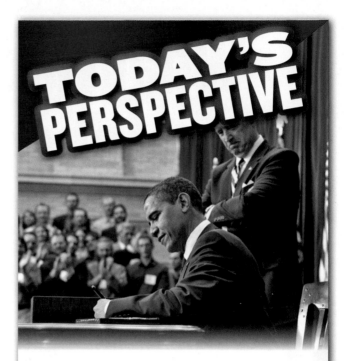

TODAY'S PERSPECTIVE

Upon taking office in 2009, President Barack Obama inherited the worst economic crisis since the Great Depression. That year, to help improve the economy and put people back to work, he signed into law the American Recovery and Reinvestment Act. In it he earmarked more than $25 billion toward environmental efforts.

During his presidency, the use of solar and wind power has increased, the nation's dependence on foreign sources of oil has been reduced, and hundreds of thousands of new jobs have been created through industries that focus on making environmentally friendly products.

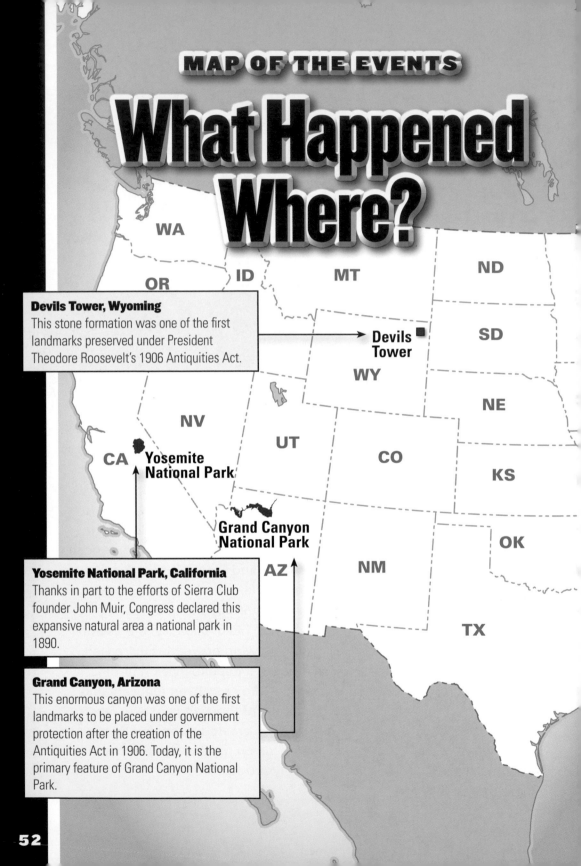

What Happened Where?

WA

OR

ID

MT

ND

SD

Devils Tower, Wyoming
This stone formation was one of the first landmarks preserved under President Theodore Roosevelt's 1906 Antiquities Act.

Devils Tower

WY

NE

NV

UT

CO

KS

CA

Yosemite National Park

Grand Canyon National Park

OK

Yosemite National Park, California
Thanks in part to the efforts of Sierra Club founder John Muir, Congress declared this expansive natural area a national park in 1890.

AZ

NM

TX

Grand Canyon, Arizona
This enormous canyon was one of the first landmarks to be placed under government protection after the creation of the Antiquities Act in 1906. Today, it is the primary feature of Grand Canyon National Park.

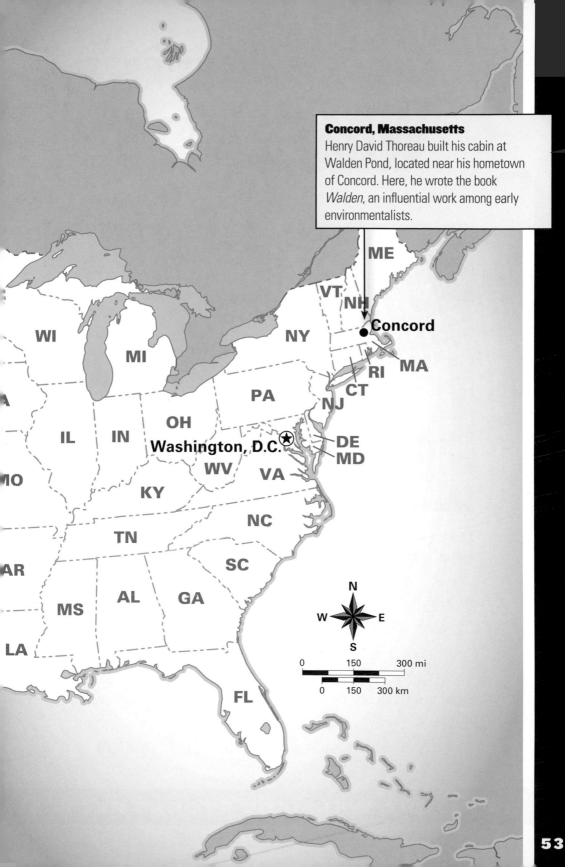

Concord, Massachusetts
Henry David Thoreau built his cabin at Walden Pond, located near his hometown of Concord. Here, he wrote the book *Walden*, an influential work among early environmentalists.

ME

VT

NH

Concord

WI

NY

MI

MA

RI

PA

CT

NJ

OH

IL

IN

Washington, D.C.

DE

MD

WV

VA

MO

KY

TN

NC

AR

SC

MS

AL

GA

LA

FL

N

W

E

S

0   150   300 mi

0   150   300 km

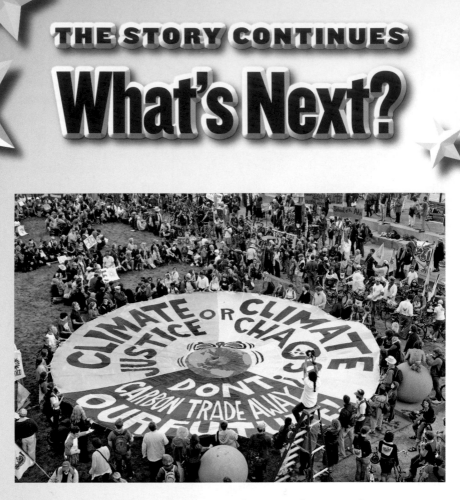

The environmental movement continues to focus on important issues such as climate change.

By the beginning of the 2000s, the environmental movement had slowed down, and public support had diminished. Some believe this is because there is no longer a clear message as to what the environmental movement is trying to accomplish. There are many different environmental groups these days. Each has its own goals. This has made it difficult to think of environmental protection as a single, organized effort. Public interest has also been hurt by the fact that the environmental movement became too political. Many people believe that environmentalists spend more time talking about solutions than making them happen.

What might be most surprising is the fact that some big businesses now seem to be taking the lead. Walmart, for example, has worked to lower its output of greenhouse gases and to make its stores more energy efficient. Is this the future of environmental protection? Will more organizations that were once part of the problem now become part of the solution? Only time will tell. But perhaps it hints at the true solution: that if we work at protecting the environment together, we will discover benefits we never dreamed possible.

Walmart is one of several large companies working to become more environmentally friendly.

OVER 80 PERCENT OF THEIR WASTE.

INFLUENTIAL INDIVIDUALS

John Muir

George Perkins Marsh (1801–1882) was the author of the 1864 book *Man and Nature*, the first major work on environmentalism.

Henry David Thoreau (1817–1862) was the author of the 1854 book *Walden*, which chronicled his nearly two-year stay in a cabin he built along the shores of Walden Pond in Massachusetts.

John Muir (1838–1914) was a naturalist and author who wrote many books and articles about his experiences in nature. He also helped found the Sierra Club and was its first president.

Theodore Roosevelt (1858–1919) was the 26th president of the United States and a passionate conservationist who created the U.S. Forest Service and designated more than 200 million acres (80 million ha) of land for protection.

Gifford Pinchot (1865–1946) served as head of the U.S. government's Division of Forestry under Presidents William McKinley and Theodore Roosevelt. Many of Pinchot's ideas were used by Roosevelt in his environmental policies.

Franklin D. Roosevelt (1882–1945) was the 32nd president of the United States. He made many political moves to support and improve the American environment, including the creation of the Civilian Conservation Corps.

Rachel Carson (1907–1964) was a biologist who wrote the landmark 1962 book *Silent Spring*, which outlined the devastating effects that pesticides—and, in a broader sense, big business—had on the environment.

Richard M. Nixon

Richard M. Nixon (1913–1994) was the 37th president of the United States. In 1970, he created the Environmental Protection Agency. He also signed into law the 1969 Endangered Species Conservation Act.

Jimmy Carter (1924–) was the 39th president of the United States. He supported the study and development of environmental initiatives, including renewable energy technologies.

Jimmy Carter

Al Gore (1948–) was the 45th vice president of the United States. He is a longtime advocate of numerous environmental issues. He is also credited with playing a key role in bringing the issue of global warming to widespread public attention.

TIMELINE

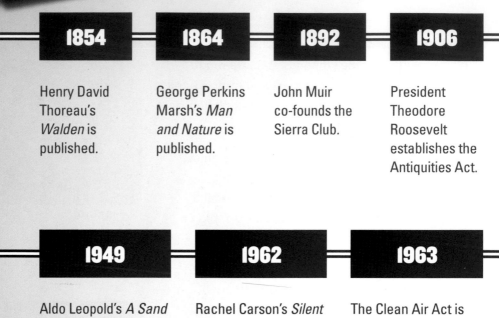

1854

Henry David Thoreau's *Walden* is published.

1864

George Perkins Marsh's *Man and Nature* is published.

1892

John Muir co-founds the Sierra Club.

1906

President Theodore Roosevelt establishes the Antiquities Act.

1949

Aldo Leopold's *A Sand County Almanac* is published.

1962

Rachel Carson's *Silent Spring* is published.

1963

The Clean Air Act is passed.

1970

April 22
The first Earth Day is observed.

July 9
Environmental Protection Agency is created by President Richard M. Nixon.

1985

Industrial nations meet in Vienna to discuss the ozone layer.

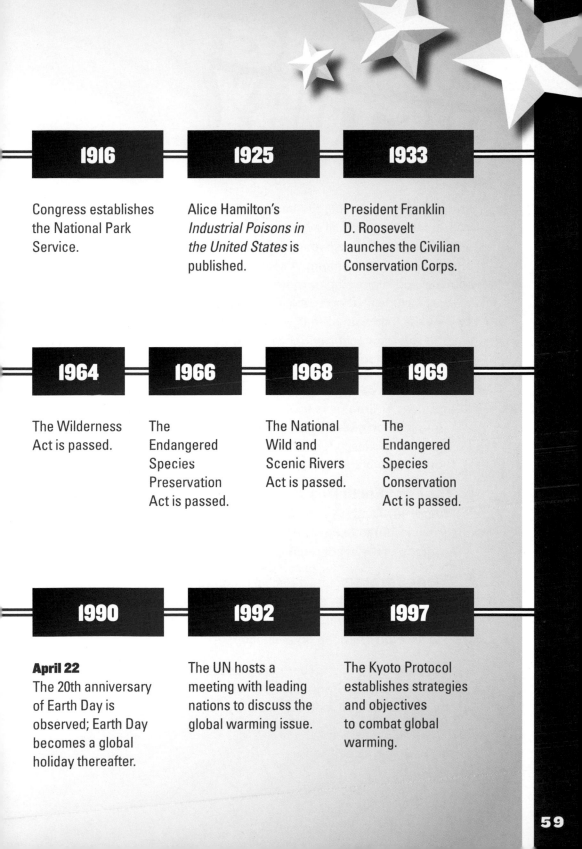

1916

Congress establishes the National Park Service.

1925

Alice Hamilton's *Industrial Poisons in the United States* is published.

1933

President Franklin D. Roosevelt launches the Civilian Conservation Corps.

1964

The Wilderness Act is passed.

1966

The Endangered Species Preservation Act is passed.

1968

The National Wild and Scenic Rivers Act is passed.

1969

The Endangered Species Conservation Act is passed.

1990

April 22
The 20th anniversary of Earth Day is observed; Earth Day becomes a global holiday thereafter.

1992

The UN hosts a meeting with leading nations to discuss the global warming issue.

1997

The Kyoto Protocol establishes strategies and objectives to combat global warming.

LIVING HISTORY

Primary sources provide firsthand evidence about a topic. Witnesses to a historical event create primary sources. They include autobiographies, newspaper reports of the time, oral histories, photographs, and memoirs. A secondary source analyzes primary sources, and is one step or more removed from the event. Secondary sources include textbooks, encyclopedias, and commentaries. To view the following primary and secondary sources, go to www.factsfornow.scholastic.com. Enter the keywords **Environmental Protection** and look for the Living History logo Σ.

Σ Al Gore's Testimony on Global Warming Former vice president Al Gore gave testimony to the U.S. Senate Environment Committee on global warming. Gore has been one of the leading voices on this issue for decades. You can watch a video of C-SPAN's coverage of the testimony online.

Σ The First Earth Day The first Earth Day celebration took place in April 1970 and was considered an overwhelming success for the environmental movement. You can watch a video of CBS's coverage of the event online.

Σ *Silent Spring* Biologist Rachel Carson's book *Silent Spring* called attention to the ways chemical companies were harming the environment and lying to the public about their actions. You can read excerpts from the book online.

Σ *Walden* Henry David Thoreau's *Walden* was a major inspiration for many early environmentalists in the United States. The entire book is available to read online.

Books

Anderson, Michael. *Pioneers of the Green Movement: Environmental Solutions*. New York: Britannica Educational Publishing, 2013.

Nakaya, Andrea. *What Is the Future of Solar Power?* San Diego: ReferencePoint Press, 2013.

Nakaya, Andrea. *What Is the Future of Wind Power?* San Diego: ReferencePoint Press, 2013.

Oxlade, Chris. *Global Warming*. Mankato, MN: Smart Apple Media, 2012.

Visit this Scholastic Web site for more information on environmental protection: www.factsfornow.scholastic.com Enter the keywords Environmental Protection

GLOSSARY

agricultural (ag-ruh-KULCH-uh-rul) having to do with farming

colonies (KAH-luh-neez) territories that have been settled by people from another country and are controlled by that country

conservationists (kon-sur-VAY-shun-ists) people who believe in the practice of managing the environment so its resources can be harvested over and over

efficient (i-FISH-uhnt) working very well without being wasteful

extinction (ik-STINGKT-shun) the process of a species disappearing completely from existence

Great Depression (GRAYT di-PRESH-uhn) a period of time lasting from 1929 until the early 1940s when the world economy was at a low, causing widespread poverty

greenhouse gases (GREEN-hous GAS-iz) gases such as carbon dioxide and methane that contribute to the warming of Earth

industrialized (in-DUHS-tree-uhl-ized) based around manufacturing companies and other businesses

lobbyists (LAH-bee-ists) people who try to influence politicians on specific issues

pesticides (PES-ti-sidez) chemicals used to kill pests, such as insects

preservationists (preh-zur-VAY-shun-ists) people who believe in the practice of keeping the wilderness free of human development or interference

radiation (ray-dee-AY-shuhn) atomic particles that are sent out from a radioactive substance

veto (VEE-toh) to stop a bill from becoming a law

INDEX

Page numbers in *italics* indicate illustrations.

ABOUT THE AUTHOR

Wil Mara is the award-winning author of more than 140 books, many of which are Scholastic titles for students.